North Cape

Selected poems of a poet turned philosopher

Robert M. Ellis

Printed and distributed by Lulu.com

ISBN 978-1-4475-5186-7

Philosophy books by Robert Ellis

A Theory of Moral Objectivity

A New Buddhist Ethics

The Trouble with Buddhism

Truth on the Edge

Also see website www.moralobjectivity.net

Contents

Introduction

This book contains a selection of poems from the whole of my life from ages seventeen to around forty. It is largely a retrospective selection, in recognition of the fact that poetry was much more important to me at earlier stages of my life than it is now. The passion which I used to put into poetry now goes largely into philosophy, for the latter has gradually and increasingly taken over from the former. This does not mean that I will never write poetry again. Who knows, the process may yet be reversed!

I see the goals of the best poetry and the best philosophy as being very similar. Poetry should speak to our experience and lead us to re-examine it afresh. Philosophy helps us to examine our beliefs and consider their justification. In both cases we should be led to re-consider things that we have been taking for granted, and thus address conditions a little more closely. Just as poetry works best when it has "something to say" – a new angle from which to consider experience – so philosophy works best when it is not just analytic, but actually offers new theoretical insights.

So my gradual move from poet to philosopher (by way of Buddhism, scholarship,
music, and a variety of other aspirations) does not seem to me to be an incongruous one. I like to think that each has supported the other, without too much intrusive interference. However much I channel my energies more towards philosophy, I do not feel too much in danger of that complete atrophying of the poetic awareness that Darwin complained of in his old age, following too much scientific analysis. My philosophy is not, nor ever will be, completely analytic. Philosophy must be geared towards the needs of practical experience, and that means that it must hold a spontaneous and imaginative poetic awareness in tension with other kinds of more rationally controlled awareness. Philosophical insights need to come from somewhere deeper than an appeal to social convention.

Putting together a selection of my poems at a time when I have almost ceased to write poetry is an odd exercise, but I have also found it an exciting one. Above all it has been a good way of connecting with my previous experiences and the variety of influences that formed my attitudes. I have also found it interesting how much more objectively I can look at my work now than I could in my early twenties when a great deal of my output was created. Digging out old files of poems, I have found a good deal of rubbish that I probably used to believe was good, and some poems that I had completely forgotten I ever wrote, that now I would rate higher than I probably did at the time. So what is included here is what I consider the best from the whole of my poetry-writing life, all of it imperfect, but all also having something to say.

The imperfections that are more obvious to me now tend to particularly afflict my earlier work. There is sometimes a straining after ecstasy in some poems, that earlier readers have remarked on. On some occasions abstract nouns interpose themselves in a way that some have found preachy, or during another phase, my use of symbolism was just too self-indulgently opaque. However, I have not attempted to completely purge the collection of these vices, as they come mixed with virtues. You may find some alarming abstract nouns, but you will also find plenty of concrete ones that arise directly from my experience. A straining after ecstasy is also an experience – sometimes one arising from an experience of ecstasy. There is always a risk that symbolism will not be understood, but up to a point, not quite understanding is part of the exploratory experience of reading poetry.

The strengths I find (and can distance myself from when it seems that I am reading the work of a past self) are those of distilling a complex or subtle experience into imagery. The poems on meditation that are included, for example, are ones I had completely forgotten ever writing until I re-discovered them, and seem to illustrate this strength. The meditation experiences they arise from are no longer a matter of regular experience (I regret to say), though I do know what they are talking about.

The wonders of publishing through Lulu mean that I do not have to offer any estimation of the market for this book in order to convince a publisher to give me the privilege of making it available. I have no idea who, if anyone, will want to read these poems. I would just like to offer them because it seems that they might possibly be meaningful, perhaps even enjoyable or inspiring, to some people somewhere. I would like to celebrate the rise of incremental publishing that makes this possible. There is now a Middle Way between the discontinuous hurdle of the publisher's approval on the one hand, and the delusions of 'vanity' publishing on the other.

Some of the poems here have been published before, the majority not. The majority of those that have been previously published were in two of the anthologies of *Virtue without Terror*, the Cambridge University Poetry Society. A couple of others have been published in *The FWBO Poetry Anthology*, a collection of poems by Western Buddhists.

Anyone who is interested in my philosophical work will find hints of it here, but not much more than that. I have not written poems about the Middle Way as a concept, for example, but, like any other poet, just written about my experience. Just occasionally experience and concept meet, for example in *Reverie during a concert in King's College Chapel:*

> ...I can be polyphony:
> the sounding out of hard and soft
> that rings into the realness
> of a clear stone cry re-echoing.

If that reminds you of the Middle Way, I will have achieved some of my purpose, but if it doesn't, then you can probably still engage with the poem in other ways.

Rather than philosophy, you will find more evidence here of my long entanglement with Buddhism. This is not only found in the section on meditation, but in the number of poems written on Buddhist retreats, and even in a couple which are about Buddhist iconographical figures. The two retreat centres of Vajraloka and Padmaloka have provided by far the best places in my experience for writing poetry. The two poems about Buddhist iconography ('Vajrasattva' and 'The Five Wisdoms') will need some gloss for those without any experience of Buddhist iconography. I have tried to provide this in the separate introduction to these two poems.

The convention that usually applies to books of poetry is that poems should always speak entirely for themselves, without any surrounding explanation or gloss, or even (often) any discernable method in the ordering. I can see much virtue in not encumbering a poem and leaving the reader to engage with it in his/her own way. However, it seems to me that a *book* of poems is a slightly different animal from poems taken singly. My feeling is that it might help people to access a book of poems if they have some sort of guiding narrative or ordering, rather than just an apparently random assortment of poems speaking for themselves in differing voices.

With that thought in mind, I have divided this book into themes, and within each theme you may also find some degree of chronological or thematic progression. I have also added an introduction to each theme giving some idea of the autobiographical background, or other points that might help understanding of the poems. All glosses are confined to these theme introductions. If you prefer the poems to speak entirely for themselves, all you have to do is ignore these introductions and go straight to the poetry.

Robert M. Ellis
Malvern, March 2011

Places

It has been places that have most frequently inspired my poetry, and that seem most symbolically important, so it is with these I begin. Of course, the places themselves are only one aspect of what I am writing about – the subject is my experience in these places. The places themselves range from Britain to Norway to South Asia to Greece.

The initial poem, *Auggedalen*, still seems to me the most important poem I have written. It celebrates my experience in the valley of Auggedal, in the Uppland Fylke near Lillehammer in southern Norway, when I was working there on a farm at the age of nineteen. As I would describe it now, I experienced intense temporary integration and meaningfulness in a way that I associated strongly with the landscape of the valley. As I described it then, I was undergoing an experience of conversion and feeling connected with God in the world. The poem is structured in terms of the different levels of the landscape in the valley, working up from the stream at the bottom to the sky at the top. You may or may not be irritated by the number of abstract nouns, but the main purpose of the poem is to communicate the sense of joy that accompanied this experience.

After my stay in southern Norway, I cycled up the length of Norway to the North Cape, often conventionally seen as the most northerly point in Europe. *North Cape* marked the completion of that rather quixotic journey, which in many ways was a quest to prove myself physically as a young man, a self-imposed initiation into maturity.

The next five poems are all concerned with experiences in South Asia. At university (at Cambridge) I studied Indian languages as well as English and Religious Studies for my first degree. During the summer vacations for three years running I managed to get travel grants to travel to South

Asia in connection with my studies. The first two poems here are about my time in Nepal in 1987. Svayambhunath Temple is a large stupa (pointy Buddhist monument) on a hill above the city of Kathmandu, whilst Muktinath is at the end of a trekking trail into the mountains, and also a point of Hindu pilgrimage. The latter site is associated with Shiva and *Muktinath* roughly translates as 'temple of freedom' or 'place of enlightenment'. Pilgrims traditionally bathe themselves in the 108 taps. However, when I reached Muktinath my mind was at least as much on a girl back in England as it was on spiritual freedom.

The next three poems are also concerned with my trip in the summer of 1988, which was to prove quite dramatic. I set out to spend a year in India studying at the University of Allahabad. However, I fled after a few days (as recorded in *Fleeing from Allahabad*) – a decision which could be excused in various ways, but I now look back on as a failure of courage. Before returning to the UK, however, I travelled in Nepal, Burma, Thailand, and Sri Lanka, spending some of the money apportioned to my year in India. Pokhara Lake is a large lake next to Nepal's second city of Pokhara, where I did go boating.

Whilst in Burma, however, I was caught up in the ultimately failed revolution against the military government, which broke out on 8th August (the significant date of 8/8/88). There was unrest throughout Burma led by monks and students, and troops fired live rounds into crowds of demonstrators. Ultimately the military government conceded elections, but did not allow the democratic movement that won them (led by Aung San Suu Kyi) to take office. My week in Burma (only a week being allowed on my visa) was an exciting one, though I never got directly caught up in the conflict. The *Schwedagon Pagoda* poem records the atmosphere in Rangoon just before these events broke out. Schwedagon Pagoda is a massive golden structure on a hill above Rangoon, surrounded by an amazing diversity of smaller stupas.

The next three poems take us back to the UK. *Iona* is one of the earliest poems in the collection, written when I was only eighteen. Iona, an island off the coast of the Isle of Mull in the inner Hebrides, is the reputed landing place of St Columba, the saint who came to convert Scotland to Christianity and set up a community on Iona. The Iona community has been refounded in modern times by George Macleod, and the island of Iona is also still a place of pilgrimage. It is alternatively known as Inchcolmkill.

King's College Chapel is the well-known chapel attached to the Cambridge College. As a Cambridge student and subsequently as a resident of Cambridge for a further year, I regularly attended concerts there. Vajraloka is a Buddhist retreat centre in Wales specialising in meditation retreats.

After a year spent living in a Buddhist community in Cambridge, in 1990 I went to the town of Veria in northern Greece to teach English. In the spring of 1991 I climbed the 8,000 foot Mount Olympus with a friend – rather prematurely given that there was still a good deal of snow on the top and we had no mountaineering equipment or experience. The approach to Mount Olympus from Litohoro is via a beautiful canyon which for me was the scene of more rapturous experiences similar to those I had had in Norway. On ascending the mountain I was also struck by the banding of landscape into forest, alpine meadow and finally snow. *Mount Olympus* is partly about my experiences there but also partly about my (as it proved, temporary) withdrawal from Buddhism. Dhaulagiri is a mountain in Nepal which can be seen from the vicinity of Pokhara.

The final poem in this section, *Buchenwald*, marks my visit to one of the former Nazi concentration camps, as recollected later at Padmaloka retreat centre. There really are the remains of a miniature zoo, including bear pits, for the amusement of SS officer's families, just beyond the perimeter wire.

Auggedalen

Stream

Shrinking of flowing age on the water's skin
wrinkling and unwrinkling swells and dies,
groans over pebbles, water led
like an old nag in the dale's bottom.
Stricken by earth-power, foam-surged by flow,
fire-crazed souls stood in chariots
and lashed the smooth back
by the mane till the blood ran,
clotted on bay flesh as hooves stumbled
down the steep slope.
All water now: driven by their own power,
not their own directions.
The hills fold those.

From the bridge I stare and concentrate
outgatherings of waters into one:
love as I see the flow is gentle,
curving and pooling in eyes of welled darkness;
faith as it drifts deep - stone-parted
confluces form, cross in unison;
joy as it quicksilver springs,
bubble from pebble, and knows
one brook is a unity, where the cows drink
the rush grows.

Earth

On the flat land, where the spreading heavy river
dumped its thawed mud, long ago,
men with laced boots carried stones,
cursing the Jotuns who hurled
one at another, marring the field's loam,
littering fertility with pyramids.

They furrowed the brow of the ground, making it yield – crusty
belief:

reasons, not power, to sow
at the snow's melt, reap
before the flesh freezes.

Yet there were rocks in the earth
standing stubborn like statues:
ten pairs of hands could not heave them!
The horses plod wearily round,
bending the furrow,
licking the clods with their hoof-beats.

But I am weary
of this straight road, built of mud and potholes.
How do I know that it leads where I go?
Are these stones from the river, where my feet
stumble over, Where the cars push past one another?
Inside those cars, in those houses where roads lead,
in those silent worlds panelled by fresh-smelling timber,
do they think of their journey?
Is the sacrifice complete?

Meadow

Where the elk-hound plays, bouncing and fleecy
with ecstasy, barking,
and sits on his bottom and slides
through the grass, and the children, laughing,
run through the red-gold and
wade through the yellow and
make little bunches of purple, there
roll the singing banks of stretching
and ripening meadow, bright tracts
between toil-field and forest.
Here the birches weep
tender greenleaves, and horses

grow up from colthood and graze.

Here the lovers lie
knotted in intricate stems in the sunshine:
the empyrean
blesses their growing.

In this youth
I stand like the plate of a dandelion
eyeing the sun:
one day I'll be
grey seed
and the wind blows.
Upwards mad ranks of young pines
thrusting out, duck their lines.
Downwards the hand of man calls:
there the earth's dead
the sun hot
on my back.

Forest

God's-fall is steepest and loudest,
its laughter sounds deepest
where dead wood twines, fungi-finned;
man-empty but life-ashift ever
is creeping and speckling each dapple's screen.

Here's madness to understand:
three norns, needles clicking,
branches shift like arms, heads
sway with belief, lichened
with grandmother's beards.

Flee! Follow the path where the light leads!
Up!
Let the barb-boughs lash skin:
there's the path

trod by twenty-years-past men
or elk
never seen –
only droppings of nightmares.

The path's lost:
the way's down,
grabbing birch trunks by the water's rumble.

Here as the little-cat water circles,
where the moss baskets, kingfisher flashes;
here I search truth in the swirl,
and the green-sway of new needles
crowding and outstretching, shadowing the water.
Fool, says the water, don't look at the forest,
look at the tree!

Leaves sharpen heaven, millions turn stretching
to one -
to the white-barked beauty flowing:
streams to the river mouth.

Sky

Like joy the swallow falls,
threads sky to river.
From wood to wood the rainbow binds,
arches the dale over.
Such standing sun laughs through the horse-clouds!

Water falling, sogging the earthlands,
weighting grasses, dripping melancholic
from the bowed needles.
Fear it not:
for it washes old leaves
and the cases of creatures,
all, from the tree's definition
to time's flow below.

The cloud's ceiling closes
one movement, one meaning:
whence the wind blows,
where the stream goes.

Blue does not green the green
by its will:
the green grows in love of blue
that together they turquoise the waters –
joy-washed as I stand on the bridge.

Norway 1985

North Cape

Cumuli shed mounting, end at the latitude,
blotting the sunlight that gold-rays clear spaces,
closed behind silhouettes: only refractions
warm on the ocean's infinite coldness.

North is the perfect will, rarest of spaces,
open horizon of longitudes crowding
after horizon to Spitzbergen, brittle
as prisms smashed into shards of the vastness.

Pride crawled here like mistletoe, creeping
and clinging round fjords and recesses,
straggling the mountains where minds breathe
in serene to space the soul forward.

Now you stand pointed, mind, there's no further
art to build coracles on this cold water:
yield to the ochre sky stranding you gently
on the ragged shoreline where last names are wasted.

Norway 1985

Svayambhunath Temple, Kathmandu

Gazing from its crown I love this country.
City packed easy from mountain
to mountain stacked a vivid green with
life-bursting rice shoots. And children:
Little robed monks play frisbee
round the temple. Staring monkeys grab.

Pilgrims walk hundreds of miles barefoot
to climb these steps, giving a paisa
to each beggar. At the top a vajra.
                        Thunderbolt.
                        Energy.
                        Change.

I swig Coke from a bottle and try to understand
what is so beautiful about these people.
From the stupa all-seeing Buddha-eyes
contemplate.

Inside. Candlelight.
Rancid butter smell.
Carefully couched books, muffled.
Bodhisattva big-eyed and naive. Laid-back monks.
Nobody cares if I wear shoes or not.

Sunset. On my way down
I toss a rupee to a beggar.
I never give money to beggars - makes them bigger beggars.
I catch his eye and he smiles at me.

Nepal 1987

Muktinath

Here in a circle of hedges,
A high clear garden
far in the desert
Himalayas, Shiva freed himself from

YOU, changeable death.
Endless thought without touch.
Music without dancing.
Words without meaning.

One hundred and eight
taps. I bathe cold in snow-sweat,
counting my frozen agony beneath
each. Ascetic. Rinsed.

Purity distrusted.
True words born in lies.
Minds free as mountains:
bodies caged.

Understanding change, Shiva sought absolute.
Endless touch without thought.
Dancing without music.
Meaning without words.

How can I chain love?

Om namah Shivaya.

Nepal 1987

Fleeing from Allahabad

A cheap Indian string bed. No net.
Mosquitoes whining through the sweated
diarrhoea-punctuated night.

I could not live in ugliness like this
Even I, the student of India's secrets, failed

and left on the morning bus to Benares,
vomiting from the window, suddenly become
a tender white man.

Padmaloka 2003 (recalling events from 1988)

Pokhara Lake

I labour to comprehend the lake's whole shore,
rounding the points between each mouth
of sparked stream from the mountains quenched,
I work to understand its calm embrace.

Between the firing sun and water's gulf,
alone in a boat too big
to paddle from the cutting
interface of life and death

I could dive, in a warm rush of cold
hugged by placidity let
forgetfulness I ever had a mother
soothe the fears away,

or lie on cracked wood, dropping
paddle, spit on sore hands,
cast off my shirt and let my lover's fire
dry moist skin to dust.

But I work still, a dead, unheeding
man across the endless interface:
wishing I was the sun who golds the lake
or the lake, comprehending sun.

Nepal 1988

Schwedagon Pagoda, Rangoon, 6th August 1988

Gold!
Pointing,
tapering
into infinity
and around are
fashioned a hundred
expectant pagodas
in opulent intricacy
clustered like disciples round
the Buddha. And you can wander endlessly
through these many palaces where there dwell
a thousand Buddhas, some reclining relaxed:
others sitting up with surprised expressions.
At their knees are the devotees bringing
ten thousand flowers and sticks of incense cooling
a hundred thousand cares in fragrant meditation. Outside
you can look out at the swarming city spread about
with a million different kinds of happiness and wretchedness.
Somewhere down there standing tense waiting in the shade at every street-corner
are the soldiers with machine-guns at their shoulders loaded with a billion bullets for the confrontation.

Iona

Waters, tarnished by sand of silk and iron,
vein-blue and venerable,
princess-woven turquoise, glassy as the sand
wrinkled by Columba's ancient anchor.

Mounds swell like waves and arch
beneath this island-ship, cross-masted
and curve-prowed, mist-worn by seas,
sailing by pillars of petrified faith.

Inchcolmkill's battlemented rock
- black, bitter piety overlain with doves' lawns -
defends self by uniqueness,
sacred peace by a spear-king's mound.

Tobermory 1984

Reverie during a concert in King's College Chapel

Pale copies are the angels of the buttresses
of those who hover in the high polyphony
beneath the delicately woven stone-webbed
arches, listening. And I too am still a pale copy

of the realness of singing. Listening
on a hard bench - then I'm soft. Listening
to hunger begging - then I'm hard. And longing
for the crying of a woman, then my cry is still

a pale copy. I can be polyphony:
the sounding out of hard and soft
that rings into the realness
of a clear stone cry re-echoing.

Cambridge 1988

Vajraloka

The hulled hills are winter-green
and coldly ripe:
round with sleeping earth
that roots the leafless trees.
Their cold is warmth
like the old age of a child.

Vajraloka 1988

Mount Olympus

I.

None of the chronicles have told us
if the Buddha ever knew snow;
though perhaps, as a young man
wandering high in Himalayan valleys
he may have gasped at the stark
flaming white crest of Dhaulagiri.
So was it a dream, or the clearest vision
of the highest abodes of meditation,
when the canopied sunlight suddenly grew grey
and that remote pure substance of the gods
began to flake about his postured limbs?
Shrivelling mountain winds began to howl
about the tree-trunks, and the million
sumptuous murmuring creatures fled or perished.
All alone, the Buddha too
was clad in that wet, frozen touch.

II.

When I have climbed the canyon far enough,
I reach pine-scented uplands where the birds are singing
and the keen sun is piercing
banks of snow with patches trickling
into the reborn earth. And the primroses
huddle in their first colonies
of tenderness.

Here the travellers stop and drink
that dull grey drink that chokes the senses.
Here the coppered youths and lovely maidens feast, and cluster
in the growing shadows of the musky pines.

Then the moon rises, talking's ended, and the dance
begins, hurling and running and twisting
on the silver mountain grass, and turning
faster and faster, man and woman, girl and boy,
till they fall
and lie together, clasped in forgetfulness.
And the primrose petals are trampled
into the earth.

But as the sunrise brushes gently
through the pine needles, I look round
at all the gently breathing bodies, swelling breasts,
dishevelled hair, stained clothing, and untidy limbs.
And suddenly my vision is
a battlefield: guerillas of the gods
have sprung and massacred an innocent
section of the civilian population
and left their white blouses and unbroken palms
purple with more than wine.

III.

When Buddha left his lovely wife
with the flowing hair and the white throat
(which he bent to kiss for the last time)
and left his slumbering children with their dreams
waist-high in sunlit cornfields,
and his last glance lingered on his suite
of silky servant girls,
he did not think of love.
Only of blood was his dream, as he saw
just such a carnage worming and clawing and spattering
over their white flesh.
Many a moral politician
resigned before he took on such a load of death as this.

IV.

I did not expect the gods to be so raucous.
So I was unprepared
for the acid cold of the wind and the bleaching sun.
Boots slithered on steep snow.
Still less did I expect
shrieking abuse and peltings.

Even the summit was uncertain
in the information white-out.
The authorities have censored
clear-lit mountains and the bright Aegean,
they have banned
the smell of sap rising in the pines.
For my ineptitude they have sentenced me
to ignorance.

Veria 1991

Buchenwald

Torture cells bear photographs and flowers.
Shot through spy-holes, corpses were piled here
and burnt in ovens in this basement.
Officers collected shrunken heads.

But just beyond the wire, for SS children's
happiness, lived bears: these were the lucky prisoners.
Further off in pens still standing, rottweilers
slavered for man-flesh.

Why did I come here? To collect
grief? To feel the high of lumps in the throat?
To know that I exist
because tears spring to my eyes?

No, to maintain the doubt yet as to whether
there is evil. I could be the cleanser,
intellectual explanation
smothering the broken heads of Jews.

I could also be
the just crusader in the British tank.
There is no evil, for it lies in me
and yet there is.

Padmaloka 2003

Plants and animals

Like many poets I have often found plants and animals a convenient objective correlative to convey human emotion. At one point I wrote a lot of short poems about flowers like "I would be..." (the first here), which merely captured a moment's perception. I have selected this as the best of the bunch.

Three buds is a rather more complex poem, written in my most poetically fertile period as a Cambridge student, which combines celebratory observation of plants with sexual elements. It is probably best left to speak wholly for itself. The *Starling* reflects the difficulties I was having with human relationships at the time. *Poppies* is also about sex – but from the point of view of an older, married, poet rather than one still struggling to get to grips with sexuality.

Lambs was written during a solitary retreat at a cottage called Castell in North Wales, at a time when my daughter was still a baby. My recent fatherhood made me more sensitive to the lambs as young creatures, but this poem also reflects my long-standing feelings about the farming industry and our hypocritical exploitation of animals (the hypocrisy often bothers me more than the exploitation by itself). I have been a vegetarian all my adult life and also a vegan for much of this period.

The Iron Tree on the other hand, is much less weighted with transferred emotion than the other poems in this section. It is just a piece of symbolic fantasy written from a sense of enjoyment.

I would be
just one daffodil
risen in a field of snow.

But now pushed through the thaw
is a galaxy of yellow.

Cambridge 1988

Three Buds

Leaf

Carefully veined and delicate stretching first
as the wings of a butterfly, then

pulsing sap fast that can
unwrap, spread his green nakedness
clean,
flag his arrogant leafness
wide
in admiring
light,

and rustling still,
grow middle-aged and brown
around the edges, crispen.
wither, seized by the breeze fall,
crunch,
decay,

all that's left of the leaf in January
is vein frail through the ice.

Blossom

Sing! For the bright petals caught
in the tree's clasp, tumbling down
as May lapses
into flower-strewn June.

Blossom's a blind hand thrust out to touch

the world's quick.
Who cares when the touch grows cold and night falls?

Like a lost limb the sense remains.

Fruit

Product of care and responsibility
you gourd yourself, swollen belly
swinging plump from a branch.
Why should everyone look after you?
The more you swell, the more they lust
for your smooth, round flesh.
But if they left you, you'd (plop!)
fall, your bruised juices fester,
you'd rot!

Cambridge 1989

The Starling

The starling's oil-bright breast
is secret-bearing plump and feather-smooth.
Somehow he's learnt the sleekness of that curve
by gliding through the winter air
and preening on the young birch bark.

Perching on the rail he looks at me,
then, like a woman, turns his back,
and, shoulders bristling, flies away.

Cambridge 1990

Poppies

unpack their baggy silks
like crumpled pantaloons expanding
crushed red out of cases,
then let it all flap
gloriously in the sun,
their massive crimson sex
revealed in the untidy careless
oiled eroticism of their skirts.

Then the autumn!
How rapidly the oiled silk dries and tatters!
In two days gone from new bloom
to an aged harlot daubed with lipstick!

If there was nature she would be
a Bombay pimp, buying and trashing
her beauties, using and expending
all for a moment's profit. So much avarice
that she can't see how glorious
our unfoldment is, and then
how cheap she makes us.

Maulds Meaburn 1999

Lambs

Charging in little gangs across the field,
they skitter, scatter, scamper tremblingly.
Meanwhile their mothers graze resignedly
in adult knowledge of the pain of things.

Their eyes now open full of tender joy:
look in those eyes again when, lambswool shorn,
they stumble from the lorry, motherless,
into the abattoir, not knowing where.

Their fear is like the first child's look of pain,
just when imagination bites the mind
with anguish of a life that's known removed,
and joy turned desperate wrenches to a cry.

The red men, fathers, in the abattoir,
will go home shaking to their anguished dreams
of desperate eyes; and on their Sundays, when
they rest, they'll teach their children to forget.

Castell 1998

The Iron Tree

Out in a sheltered bay on the west coast
lies a mild Scots village; from the kirk
a path winds through the pines beneath the cliff.
There in a dell you'll find it, like an oak
with armoured bark, that rings when struck.
No-one knows who made it: mythic heroes? men?

No Atlantic gale will break its branches,
and no worm will riddle it, no rot.
In spring the tiny silver buds will gather,
break, and grow into a gauntlet.
As the summer lengthens, tender steely leaves
will turn to pewter, crinkle, fall like
armourer's-floor filings. There the villagers
scramble for the fallen leaves to bring long life.

Padmaloka 2003

People

It has sometimes been a source of regret or shame to me that I am not a “people person”, with all the social virtues that brings with it. My participation in a Buddhist community and my work as a teacher have taught me a lot of social skills, but these have often had to be learnt the hard way rather than developing spontaneously. However, I am a human being, human beings are social animals, and I can hardly pretend that personal relationships with others have not formed an important dimension of my life.

My poetry has only occasionally been directly about people, and it is only a selection of that that is included here. Some of what I have written I am not yet ready to publish – especially poetry to, or about, my wife, who has obviously been the most important relationship in my life. However, here is a small selection of other poetry about people.

The first of these *On the death of Ivy Hawkes*, was written after the death and funeral of an elderly neighbour in my parents’ home in Luton. It is not so much about her as an individual as about death.

The next (to which I have only recently given the title *Love Poem*) reflects the exhilaration – and perhaps the delusions – of the falling-in-love moment. Again, it is not really about her (the object of my infatuation) at all, but about my feelings on falling in love. This is fairly typical of my early attitude to human relationships.

The next two poems, about my father and mother respectively, I have included particularly because they mark an effort to move beyond earlier self-absorbed attitudes. Whilst on retreat at Vajraloka I reflected on my relationships to my family, and deliberately sat down to write poems in appreciation of my father, mother, and elder sister. At the time this seemed just like a kind of spiritual exercise, and it is only now looking back at them that I see much worth in the poems themselves. The poems about my mother and father are included, because they seem to have succeeded in capturing them (in relation to me of course) in a positive light at a particular time. In reading *My father at his desk* it might be helpful to know that he has been a missionary in the Congo and a Baptist minister. I also cannot read *With my mother in the garden* now without feeling it to be a kind of belated memorial poem, as she died two years ago.

An unsuitable friendship arose from my experience as a teacher in a sixth-form college. Whilst the majority of my teaching has been of Philosophy, Religious Studies and Critical Thinking, in the earlier stages of my career I also taught English Literature (something that I very much enjoyed on the whole – though as this poem reveals, it was not entirely without its frustrations).

On the death of Ivy Hawkes

Poetry is form's loss, flesh
stiffened over a chair-back,
never to unshape. Even in April
her teenage friends retain

their round fur hats, in rows,
while the young pall-bearers
breathe vapour. As contractors
spread the town's frontiers like ripples,

her life sank like the stone:
stroking each warm-plumb-depth
in the cloudy fall, beauty slow
to the thrower's eye.

As stone hits bottom, so
ripples strive to tongue over the chalk banks,
cease, as the form loses energy, thickens:
so liquid settles and matter freezes.

Luton 1986

Love poem

Slates smash from broken Babylon!
Hear the split bricks, gentle-tendril-encurled, hurled!
Let stem rub stone, climb air,
seeing the sun's blaze!

And the half-unclenched leavelets shiver,
baring cold green in warm breezes,
till from the river's mirror ray-drawn rises
mist, and in folding showers dry searchings cease.

Cambridge 1986

My father at his desk, about twenty years ago

A shivering sound is heard behind the door
like a small gasping wind chafing the rooftops. It means work.
But inside where he sits the sun pokes through the window,
warms the study's book-lined air, and glances

on the wooden model boat from Africa that paddled
great muddy rivers, the twanging thumb-board
making alien notes, the talking drum (that speaks now
of the past), and the dense-packed shelves

of theology and history, big books on wartime
paper (maps of Belgium on the back), bibles,
hymn-books, old atlases with half the world in pink:
and in the midst he reads and writes and telephones

- what? The content did not matter, but
the form and vision and the application of it.
Some men mended roads or drank in pubs
(I barely knew) but this one worked, in humble privacy,

within the space created by his mind. In between
old ladies, river-baptisms in Congo, scribbled
notes of sermons, deacons' meetings, preaching plans
there stretched a purpose and (I later saw) a thought of love.

Vajraloka 1998

With my mother in the garden, about twenty years ago

You grew radishes that bright dry year,
spring onions and tomatoes, by the rowan tree.
Another, you put up with seven young oaks:
the beginning of a forest I was yet to plant.

The tiny red crab apples you turned into
thick sweet puree. When the willow
wept its leaves, you raked them up, and I
had nowhere left to hide.

The strawberries and I both wandered wantonly
beneath the roses. You sowed honesty
that came up purple, then in round dry flaps.
It took much longer to grow up in me.

When you were digging, turning up the soil
I wanted to dig too, but dug a hole.
I wanted to find buried treasure.
You knew better how to make it grow.

Vajraloka 1998

An unsuitable friendship

The two walk by
arms intertwined, while I
stand at the bus-stop watching
the sweep of their long blonde hair

and laughter. I find their friendship
unsuitable. The taller one, six foot and shaped
like a Barbie doll but said by her parents to be the next
Shakespeare
will infect

the shorter one with the keen eyes
with her slow arrogance and being sure
that it can't be relevant to her
and it's a waste of time really

and it doesn't matter to her if she talks
while I'm talking because her boyfriend says she has
beautiful blonde hair, though he's too possessive really, and
shaped
like the next sonnet

and of course she'll bring the essay next time,
even though she can't get quite the right colour for her hair,
and she's sorry she was talking when I was talking
and she's taking her driving test next Wednesday.

And the shorter one who used to try very hard
will be drowned in a sea shaped like Shakespeare,
floating among the water weeds like the next Ophelia
as the tendrils intertwine her blonde hair and wrap her bright
eyes.

Leigh-on-Sea 1995

Literature and art

This section contains poems that were stimulated in some way by the work of other writers or by works of art. The second and third of them are in some ways consciously derivative.

The earliest of these, *Incarnadine*, was initially stimulated by a line from Shakespeare's Macbeth: "The multitudinous seas incarnadine", spoken by Lady Macbeth as she is trying to wash the blood off her hands, and imagines that all the waters in the world would be turned red sooner than washing her hands free of blood.

In my first year at Cambridge I studied English, but as the year went on became increasingly frustrated with the subject. In particular I found the process of writing essays on works of literature increasingly blocked and difficult. One of the turning points in leading to me deciding to drop English, and take up Indian Studies instead, was when I found myself unable to write an essay about Gerard Manley Hopkins (who is perhaps my favourite poet). My liberal supervisor, John Newton, listened to my plight and then suggested that I just write any sort of response. I took him at his word and wrote a poem instead, and that poem is included here as *A tribute to Gerard Manley Hopkins*.

When I left the Buddhist community in Cambridge to go to Greece I was given a volume of the poems of Cavafy to take with me by a friend in the community. I became very fond of these. As translated into English they have a kind of anecdotal style combined with classical references that seem to make us at home in ancient Alexandria. *Black Rain* is a kind of pastiche of Cavafy, prompted by reports of black rain falling in the Middle East during the First Gulf War, due to burning oil wells.

Finally, *Angel with a vielle* records a period of passion for the Renaissance paintings to be found in the National Gallery, London. The painting is thought to be by an associate of Leonardo da Vinci, and the angel looks partially like a painting of a statue, depicted in a niche.

Incarnadine

The sea is a mind
ebbing and tiding at the moon's pull:
a dark beast, gentled by music,
turning and twirling like white dancers,
or, goaded by tridents,
raged into crashing waves like bears' paws.

Dreams are like lone fishes
lost in infinitude of cold grey,
each night trawled to a bare deck, where, bulb-eyed,
they flap in slivery defiance.

But far down in the deep
lurk uncreatures, seen only by groping
dismembered tendrils glimpsed in grey
and eyes
straining like covetous old ladies into shop windows,
and chainmailed chimeras
incisored jaws acute
as past and present tearing now.

You wake up feeling sick,dizzy:
cold salt sweat runs over you.
As if, lying on land, lips clammy and lungs out-squeezed,
you remember swimming in the deep lake that reflects the sky;
tired, choked, losing the tread of reality, struggled;
then the waters caressed you,
drawing in reveries to a slow sleep
of forgetfulness.

The nightmare that was past is still with you:
for you have swallowed the ocean
and it seethes in your head, the cauldron of the universe.
When the seas boil, steaming in tarry vapours
blackening upward to tarnish the moon:
when the condensed matter of the universe drips
from the cosmic skull,

and the dregs of the seas unwatered lie below:

that is the mind without dreams.

Luton 1983

A tribute to Gerard Manley Hopkins

As each clasped bud, gold-blown,
a round clenched earth unpalms,
and the world's ore from one
sucked bursting mound unbounds,
so each stone's word is sapped
from living juices, each dead clod
but ingrown life, a burnt fire's god.

And molten sap is lava to the foundry
where man beats heaven in hell.
By dead iron's hammer on iron
juice springs, metal timbers, life is wrought
even in pale hands that nail
flesh in tree. Risen golden:
words from stones made earths.

So man tarnished, washes bright
in river-silver. Laboured crosses
weigh free necks to ground, in clay
steel yielding, birth dissolving.
Does gold beaten light shrink faster
into hills, or darken? Love each hammer's blow:
for finger tips, that grip, are tendrils.

Cambridge 1986

Black Rain

The falling of black rain
put an end to the emperor's pretensions
that he controlled the weather.
For, as the washerwoman said,
what emperor would ever want or dare
to splash her white gowns flapping in the breeze
with grimy spots? Pure youth and beautiful
maiden alike were sullied with the black
aspersions which even cast themselves
over the white suit of that strapping young god,
Caligula, as he strode in the palace grounds.

Veria 1991

Angel with a vielle

Sad,

fine-feathered wing pressed against the stony
alcove, eyes bloated
by shadow, delicate fingers just
holding a brittle
bow to scratch
lost
music,

the folds of your green
robes
flow
in starchy curves, one foot awkwardly
poised before the other,

brushed alive

but weighted still
with the stillness of death.

Leigh-on-Sea 1995

Poetry about poetry

As a Cambridge student, one of my favourite themes for poetry was poetry itself, the process of its creation and the contradictions involved in turning experience into words. At that time I think I took poetry as a kind of spiritual calling, so this kind of poetry sometimes took the place of impulses that would later become more directly religious or philosophical. Sometimes religion and the act of poetic creation would also overlap, though, as they do here in *Easter*.

The first three poems in this section express themselves fairly directly. The first two untitled poems in this section should need no further explanation. *Easter,* too, should be able to speak for itself provided you give due weight to the title. Oddly, it now strikes me as the most Christian poem I have written in a life that has mainly involved reacting against a Christian background.

Writing poetry about poetry is often a recipe for pretentious rubbish, and I have discarded quite a bit of this. Much of what I wrote at this time (in the late eighties) involves opaque symbolism for the act of writing poetry. Of this kind of poem, I have left only *Poem for poets* in this section. This does still seem to me to have something to say, though it says it in something of the tone of a Dali painting. It would not be helpful, I think, to try to gloss what it is trying to say. It will either speak to you in some way as it is, or it will not.

If I write on the thinnest of papers
its crisp delicacy does not rustle
like a poppy shaking.

The beauty if perfume could express;
if words could become petals!.
But they fall in the mud.
They leave bald stamens.

I do not want crushed poppies.

Cambridge 1986

The page my lover
draws each secret, drains
my spilling vessel,
listens to each death
and bears again.

But I don't listen
to her advice,
cannot bear
her blank looks,
hate her open
love.

Cambridge 1986

Easter

THE OBJECT OF POETRY IS TO KILL WORDS

I begin with it
which is not a word
and pushing, pulling, gently cajoling
nurture it
into a word
which is not it.
And you, reader,
taking a knife
slit the word
from navel to gullet:

and the ground is drenched
with its blood,
the soil is nourished
with its flesh,
the rocks ground
with its bones:
and in the end
it is earth.

THE OBJECT OF POETRY IS TO BECOME REAL

This poem is dead already:
its face is a man you once loved
neatly coffined so his stench
cannot rise
and the terrible grip of his
otherness cannot get out define himself and seize you.
Locked in box and earth,
sealed in his symbol, how can this dead man live?

THE OBJECT OF POETRY IS TO LOVE

I begin with earth
and start to dig
to find out where this fragrance rises:
broken pots, rotten
roots, bones?

Nightfall. I leave.
But when my back turns in the dim light
small sprouts begin to curl and turn in liberated life;
tendrils dancing climb the air
in ecstasy.
And suddenly the moonlit world is filled
with fine perfume.

Cambridge 1988

Poem for poets

Those days are pumped like flesh
out of an elephant skin:
then you stand back
watching it deflate
sensually.

While the stretched drum-skin
wrinkles and crumples
turn and watch
the mound of stinking life
as vultures beak
the straggling veins.

Cry out, cry out
to ringing trees and stones
and vultures
which flap off, digested.

Then remember:
such a glass globe does not crack,
but like a lamp whose flame flares up too fine
it smashes.

Cambridge 1987

Meditation

I have struggled to practise meditation through most of the period in which these poems were written, since I was first taught it by Buddhists in my first year at university. It has often been helpful to me, though in ways that were not always immediately apparent at the time. The days when any kind of fulfilling experience has arisen from meditation have been vastly outnumbered by the days when I got up from it in restlessness and frustration. However, those moments when meditation has gone more deeply have been worth the effort.

It is a cliché of meditation practice to say that one does not do meditation to have meditation experiences. One does meditation, instead, to have an incremental effect on one's habitual mental states. Perhaps, in my case, I do it just to try to keep open a window showing the possibility of relaxed aesthetic awareness as an alternative to any rigid beliefs or inflexible emotional states I might fall into.

Nevertheless, the poems included here were generally prompted to some degree by "meditation experiences". They do seem to me to communicate something about those experiences, which may aid in the appreciation of some aspects of meditation, provided these limitations are remembered. I probably need to write a lot more poetry about the frustrations of meditation as a counterpoint to these celebratory poems.

Sonnet comes from very early in my encounter with meditation, and has a Christian flavour. *Breath*, on the other hand, probably arises from reflections associated with the mindfulness of breathing, a meditation practice in which one focuses on the process of breathing.

High Wind was written during a meditation retreat at Vajraloka, following the experience of sitting in a shrine hall in meditation while a high wind blew outside. In these sorts of circumstances the weather conditions can almost seem to merge with the fabric of one's consciousness. The association of breathing with wind is also central here.

Meditation is straightforwardly an attempt to express an absorbed meditative state through imagery.

Sonnet

I'm doing this for him I said I would
Because he crafts the whole and knows the fall
from reason into action. His the form
for broken words, dream-killing letters, images
torn from the whole to form new prayers: trees
built from the broken and chopped bits up, and burned.

And no more reasons, parts of reasons, help
me see the green sand where there are no more.
Concentrate the clean act, act itself is reason:
willow's act in growing by the stream.

Risen act, tree-straight, leaf-curled at the form's end
gathers inward reasons reined on vein ends:
Slowed as the sap shrinks, rain respires
out to the cold air, riven in silence.

Cambridge 1986

Breath

Old age is taught
like the lighting of a fire
and each breath is fought
like the gutting of a wick.

But to free youth in the blood;
that is hard like the knot
of my own vein. To loose it
breaks the water-bringing rope.

I draw from the well
and take deep draughts, then
slack, unthirsted. Unknotted I pull
and the stone body tumbles.

Cambridge 1988

High Wind

Each rain-varnished branch and every frond are
trebly alive, to buck and shake and pitch.
Clouds gallop. Robes thrash. Even a tree-trunk
sways to the searching, pushing wind and falls.

Wind is curious and young, nose like a bullock,
fresh like a girl's face asking a question.
Energy live on the moment's edge, poised,
then like a knife passes, death in its wake.

When life flows out the wind of breath takes leave.
High in the blue blown heavens I will pass
forcing my way through azure Viking-like
and having ransacked with the wind, disperse.

Vajraloka 1997

Meditation

A silver tension stills
between the water's gulf and air above,
holds, as the skin of milk
the fat of fearlessness.

Even a knife's blade stabbed
into a lake is suddenly enamelled
with shining mother-of-pearl
as the tension stretches,

sure as elastic armour. And my fist
grasped out into the air above runs
bright with the clarity of it.
Standing above, the fear is far

like something vague behind a mirror
while the body lying shell-clear in bare water
basks in the sunlight streaming through.
And the mud has sunk, and the silver burns.

Cambridge 1988

Frustration

The poems in this section have arisen from various kinds of 'negative' states, whether these are of confinement, anguish, physical pain, or hatred. It has always seemed to me a legitimate function of poetry to express our experience of these things. Ultimately, I would like to put such experiences in a more optimistic wider frame, but it is also important not to move on to that more positive frame too hastily. A dark poem too quickly laid aside (whether it is one's own or someone else's) may be an opportunity for the acknowledgement of dark emotions lost.

At the age of eighteen I attended an Arvon Foundation creative writing course, mainly with older people. At the end of this course there was a celebratory evening where we all read poetry. After a number of light poems, with the assembled company becoming quite jolly, I still remember reading out Donne's *Nocturne upon St Lucie's Day*, a wonderfully melancholy poem. This is still something I do not regret doing, though perhaps it required a certain amount of social insensitivity at the time.

The first of the darker poems included here, *The walls are high on either side…* was written when I was seventeen, and still speaks to me of adolescent confinement. *Snapped-off poem,* a few years later, can speak best for itself of a specific type of anguish. *Cam in November* was written at one of many times of loneliness and frustration in Cambridge.

Hospital Haiku, on the other hand, were prompted by the biggest experience of physical pain in my life so far, after I suffered a compound fracture in both bones of one ankle in a bicycle accident. These haiku were written some weeks after my stay in hospital, on a creative writing retreat at Padmaloka. In the tradition of haiku, each one is self-contained and attempts to capture a moment of insight, often one of impermanence.

Cain reflects my experiences of ingrained, apparently unshiftable hatred following my resignation from a teaching post at a college due to conflicts with the principal and some other colleagues. There are moments in our lives when positive thinking fails, and when the conditions in the world, or in our psyches, just cannot be easily turned in a positive direction. It seems to me that the best we can do is just to acknowledge these moments as fully as we can, and then move on from them.

The walls are high on either side,
the road is smoothed, the walls are bared,
the way eternal: dumbly funnelled.
The walls are high on the either side:
and so I run from scarlet side to side.
They're on their side.
Walls insurmountable, highway sempiternal,
bald as ice-blocks, they stand irredoubtable.

Luton 1983

Snapped-off poem

Stacks of awareness unbearable
stick from the mud like snapped-off
piles of a pier now storm-crushed driftwood. The body has
freedom:
split into lone planks or moving
islands held by rusty nails and greased by soggy sea. But
limbs stand
broken, aching nerve-ends.

Cambridge 1988

Cam in November

River nearly overflows its banks.
Swans dip heads deep and drag
pain by the roots from a muddy bed.
Here's an ugly woman with a pretty child.

Swan's white back shrugs
wind and mud and overflow.
But her head snakes down too deep and up.
I wring the swan's neck with my words.

Cambridge 1989

Hospital Haiku

I try to stand and
my right foot swivels sideways:
it's no longer me.

The ambulanceman
cuts off my sock with scissors:
I shall not need it.

My daughter sees my
purple foot and starts to cry:
it's her who suffers.

Jocund nurse perches
toy parrot on her shoulder:
now gloom and stress lift.

The desperate old man
cries again and again for help:
I need it less.

After a long day's
thirst, sweat and pain comes relief:
anaesthesia.

I try out crutches
in underpants down the hall:
brazen, I don't care.

Padmaloka 2003

Cain

The preacher's life-blood went into his sermon,
while the congregation fiddled and dreamed.

The teacher with red care had bled herself
for forty years, but from the final brood
of texting teenagers relieved to fly,
no chocolates came, nor cards, nor even looks:
what recompense polite applause from scarce-born
colleagues, or the proffered handshake,
next to this stab of hate, what next?

He reared that lamb as though it was his son,
but God, the busy publisher, did not return the call.

The murderous philosopher had built
his city up with care: the gates of bronze
fine-wrought, the walls deep-founded and the whole
sharply defended by tight argument. But now the guards
rot at their posts, unread, the undebated streets
grow weeds, while spineless new white suburbs
of the doomed living cities are packed out with praise.

So he plunged his rage into his brother tiller,
smashing the fat complacent cities of the plains.

Worcester 2006

Transformation

In the longer term, I would like to see the frustration in the previous section in a context of transformation. Transformation accepts negative or destructive experience in order to build something greater out of it. The poetry of transformation is greater than the poetry of frustration because it takes that further step, from acknowledgement to transformation. It is difficult to get right because, if the transformation is not expressed fully enough, it may seem to be stuck in the acknowledgement of frustration. On the other hand, if the transformation is emphasised too much over the frustration, the transformation may seem too superficial. The successful poetry of transformation expresses the Middle Way by balancing both requirements whilst doing justice to both.

I am not sure to what extent the three poems included here are successful poems of transformation, but at least they can stand as attempts. *Peace is a glass jar* suggests transformation in rather a compressed way, and *On the fallen oaks near Vajraloka* is more of a reflection on impermanence. Perhaps it is the cheerfulness with which it considers impending dissolution that makes it also seem to me about transformation. *Changing waters* develops the transformatory theme more explicitly.

Peace is a glass jar:
when moments shatter its brightness
splinters
and those dead shards
piecing again glass new.

Lit in glass cases those vessels
bruised in a thousand colours
fill again the angry breaker
with the thirst of shattered waters.

One clear light is broken, not its cleaver.

Cambridge 1987

On the fallen oaks near Vajraloka

Two great oaks
still lie fallen from last winter's storm.
Massive trunks
block the track
and a great bunched ball of roots
is wrenched from the earth.

No slow gnawing movement took you,
not like the wind carving
the rocks into weird shapes in the desert,
nor like the river chiselling gorges
between two mountains: nothing slow,

but a huge thwack of wind
undid your might in one great
push, as if the restless hill itself stood up,
took hold of you and knocked you prone
with a casual flick.

So one day this solid house, my skeleton,
void and deserted, choked by weeds
and pigeons but (it seems) still whole,
when a bird's foot rattles a stone will suddenly
cave with a mountainous crash.

And my bones will lie like upwrenched trunks
and the vision grown by my heart's branches
stick upended with its mass of roots.
What we think most firm goes suddenly:
bridges, friends and doctrines. Civilisations. Me.

Vajraloka 1998

Changing Waters

Between two oceans timbers creak
and mastheads tremble, openings
of waters tumble seething brack
back into new breadths.
A screaming ship is standing on the edge of oceans
like an insect on the balance of a leaf.

Before you leave the day, night, sky and sea,
you would embrace it as you would a child.
Before you change the waters from the salt
to the fresh that know you not, he will hold
you too with clenched palms and eyes white
with the same savour: warm and brittle.

In the sunlight with the red tulips
rise deep colours from the fresh earth:
tread the ground soft and brush
your limbs on succulence.
A screaming ship is standing on the edge of oceans
like an insect on the balance of a leaf.

In these new seas the water is as sweet
as dew that's gathered in the hollow of a petal.
There it laps the encrustations from the body,
strokes with strength and wraps in coolness.
The scattered drops that glitter in the garden
are the same oceans, wept before that parting.

Cambridge 1988

Buddhism

This final section contains two culturally Buddhist poems making use of Buddhist iconography. It seems appropriate to put them at the end, after the transformation theme, because the figures of enlightenment that they celebrate represent the outcome of transformation, the ideal of enlightenment.

I have never had as close a relationship to these figures as I at one stage would have liked to cultivate. Ultimately, it seems, most Buddhist figures are not rooted deeply enough in my symbolic landscape for me to relate to them strongly. Many of them are also too remote and static, representing not the process of transformation close to our experience, but a remote outcome that is beyond our experience.

The two poems here, however, represent some of my best attempts to get to grips with those figures. *Vajrasattva* I now see mainly as a poem about meditation experience *associated* with the figure of Vajrasattva. Vajrasattva literally means something like 'Thunderbolt being' and is traditionally supposed to represent the highest distillation of pure enlightenment. Of course, in daring to associate Vajrasattva with a mere meditation experience I am turning him into something other than that – though something much more meaningful, perhaps.

The Five Wisdoms offers a poetic treatment of the Five-Buddha mandala. A mandala is a circular diagram which is traditionally supposed to show a sort of diagrammatic analysis of the elements of enlightenment. The Five-Buddha mandala does this by breaking down the qualities of enlightenment into those of four Buddhas of different colours in the four directions, unified by the fifth, white, Buddha in the centre. The four coloured Buddhas are blue Akshobya in the east, yellow Ratnasambhava in the south, red Amitabha in the west and green Amoghasiddhi in the north. Vairocana is the white Buddha in the centre. You should be able to get a sense of the qualities associated with each of these Buddhas from the poem, but for more details I can recommend *Meeting the Buddhas* by Vessantara, published by Windhorse Publications.

What fascinates me about the Five-Buddha Mandala is that it consists in dynamic relationships between different qualities. Each of the different coloured Buddhas around the edge of it must enter into a dialectical relationship with the others in order to achieve an integration of their qualities in the central white Buddha. However, in thinking about it in this way I am already taking leave of the Buddhist tradition. I am thinking of the coloured Buddhas as interestingly imperfect, subjecting their various faults along with their positive qualities to a process of greater integration; but Buddhist tradition insists on seeing all the Buddhas of the Five-Buddha mandala as perfect, and therefore static rather than dynamic figures. This poem is really an attempt to make the five Buddhas (or at least their symbolic associations) into more dynamic figures through imaginative exploration of their meaning.

Vajrasattva

You are the ice beyond the veil of breath.
You are the veins of silver in the air.
You are the stream force of water swirling.
You are the snowflake's finest fashioning.

Within a mask half-filled I see your face,
glimpsed behind the painted eye and smile,
and in the gesture brandished in your hand:
but every glimpse betrays another mask.

Through each door's chink behind I almost see
the opening to freedom, air and space,
until the door returns to wood once more,
still beaten like the panels of a dream.

Even in the mirror where I twist
about to catch your naked face, each form
reflects another and reflects again
until I see the terror of myself.

Oh Vajrasattva, that is where the silk
material knowledge then is ripped apart,
revealed the truth behind the play of masks:
I am Vajrasattva; you are me.

Vajraloka 1997

The Five Wisdoms: a cycle of poems on the Five-Buddha Mandala

1. Akshobya

In the east is a land without shadows,
where blue snow crunches underfoot.
Sharp ice razors, untouched by the unrisen
sun that sends sparse pale rays into night's end.

In the shivering wilderness wander wild
bands of philosophers, harsh and dry
with wind-blown faces, stout sticks and wearing
only loincloths. They don't feel

the cold, but when they meet
wood clashes wood and shouts
break the still air like shattered
staves. If you meet them they will give

or take anything, their thievery
impossible as their generosity.
Each one carries rattling at his waist
a rotten skull, stinking of life.

They fear nothing: snow-bears, blizzards,
blood, all are alike to them. Wine makes no mark.
Women shrivel in the white glare, and sentiments
perish in icy waste. They love not.

Each day they sit encamped back-to-back
immobile, poised in purest meditation,
the changing whirl of the wind reflected
back unchanging from their still blue eyes.

2. Ratnasambhava

On the yellow sand of the coast rings
the sea, in the air the smell of thyme.
From villages the people sail their fishing boats
in the balmy winds, and the dolphins jump.

Hauling the nets they sing as they work -
chanting on the quay, music in the fields.
In the night they dance and drink red wine,
toasting their friendships brother to brother.

In this land of jewels all the children live:
for each has enough and is given enough.
And the gold is given to all and used
to plate the rooftops, blazing in the sun.

No loneliness is here, for the old
gather to tell their stories to the young.
And the dead are followed in golden coffins,
shimmering in the happiness of grief.

Then the sun shines on the gleaming temple,
and the bell sounds deep in the heart's bond,
and the people, robed and garlanded in yellow, gather,
walking together through the cypress trees,

through the great oak doors and the massive columns
to the place where the beating drums and mantras solemn
echo and re-echo with one great voice. Then they stand
in silence, and as one before the yellow Buddha bow.

3. Amitabha

Red is the colour of deepest desire,
staining the peaches and the tomatoes,

flushed cheeks and crimson-red dresses, sunsets
blooding the ocean beyond the land's limits.

In the land of desires they are free to roam,
prowling and captivating, springing and purring,
running for ever and flying, delighting
and playing, embracing and kissing.

The red land is boundless: its groves
ever fruit; its rivers run reckless;
its springs never dry; its wharves
piled with rubies, its cities with towers.

Each one in the red land pursues his own wishes:
travelling endlessly through new worlds, sitting
in wonder upon a calm mountainside, flaming
in joyous response to the spirit within him.

In the high caves dwell the djinns
who give out to initiates magic spells:
drunk with their mastery then they can change shapes,
swallow whole cities, see the gods.

Each one then rules his own empire wrought
of his own iron, peopled by fantasy's denizens:
angels his subjects, demons his thralls,
he conquers the whole wide space of his world.

4. Amoghasiddhi

In the darkness the trees sway
in the wind and the branches bend,
keeping their rigour and holding, just as the green men
in the dark tangle of forest fearlessly tread
through their moon-lit realm, killing
and healing, taking and leaving,
forcing compassionate tracks through the growing
confusion of branches, briars and creepers.

Intent as black cats they weave their trail
under and over, mindful and silent. Searching
their prey they bend bow and the arrow leaps,
deadly unerring, straight to the heart's blood.

But then the hurt beast that comes to their healer
enters in safety, known to the wise man.
There in the night he pulls thorns from dumb creatures:
bruising of herbs fills the air with sweet scent.

By the tribe's doctors the wisdom is passed on.
Knowing the whole wood, they know the best way:
where to heed snake's poison; which trees to cut,
which spare the axe; which plants to tip

the lethal arrow, which the healing palm;
which dying man to kill and which to cure.
Under a green Buddha the doctors sit and meditate,
gathering for the time when of one mind, they speak.

5. Vairocana

Look as the rainbow clears and the sun's bright light
white shrivels the rain and beats back the dark!

Watch as the sun long hoped-for rises
in the blue ice-land with fiery splendour.
Softens the hard ice. Dribbles the snow-pack.
Flowers burst forth, and philosophers pick them.

In the yellow land the calm sun sets.
Gold glitters no more, and princes
cast their last look at their palaces,
plunging ascetic-robed into the forest.

In the red land the red sunset sinks into dusk.
Turning to telescopes each lover yearns

for the unknown and ungrasped
shining of distant stars in the darkness.

Then comes the dawn in the trackless forest,
paved with gold highways now. Will the hunter
no more pursue with fell dart the quarry.
In friendship and healing all the beasts gather.

In the temple of the sun will they all come,
to sing the praises of the many who are one.

Vajraloka/Maulds Meaburn 1998-9

www.ingramcontent.com/pod-product-compliance
Ingram Content Group UK Ltd.
Pitfield, Milton Keynes, MK11 3LW, UK
UKHW020205200726
13856UKWH00003B/1217